W9-BMX-991

AMERICAN COMMUNITIES

We Live in a
SMALL TOWN

Mary Austen

PowerKiDS press.

New York

Published in 2016 by The Rosen Publishing Group, Inc.
29 East 21st Street, New York, NY 10010

First Edition

Editor: Katie Kawa
Book Design: Reann Nye

Photo Credits: Cover, p. 21 Kenneth Sponsler/Shutterstock.com; cover, pp. 3–24 (background texture) Evgeny Karandaev/Shutterstock.com; p. 5 Tom Merton/Caiaimage/Getty Images; p. 6 (town) Sean Doug Schneider Photography/Moment/Getty Images; pp. 6 (city), 13 littleny/Shutterstock.com; p. 9 Michael Shake/Shutterstock.com; pp. 10, 24 (post office) Joseph Sohm/Shutterstock.com; p. 14 (top) Pressmaster/Shutterstock.com; p. 14 (bottom) wavebreakmedia/Shutterstock.com; p. 17 Flashon Studio/Shutterstock.com; pp. 18, 24 (town hall) DonLand/Shutterstock.com; p. 22 Sergey Novikov/Shutterstock.com; p. 24 (library) DavidPinoPhotography/Shutterstock.com.

Library of Congress Cataloging-in-Publication Data

Austen, Mary.
We live in a small town / Mary Austen.
    pages cm. — (American Communities)
Includes webography.
Includes index.
ISBN 978-1-5081-4193-8 (pbk.)
ISBN 978-1-5081-4194-5 (6 pack)
ISBN 978-1-5081-4195-2 (library binding)
1. Cities and towns—Juvenile literature. I. Title.
HT119.A97 2016
307.76—dc23
                            2015023172

Manufactured in the United States of America

CPSIA Compliance Information: Batch #BW16PK: For Further Information contact Rosen Publishing, New York, New York at 1-800-237-9932

Contents

A small town is a great place to live.

5

town

city

6

A town is a kind of urban community. A town is like a city, but it is smaller.

Many of the buildings in our town are on the same street. This street is called Main Street.

9

Our **post office** is on Main Street. This is where we go to send letters.

All the kids in our town
go to the same school.

13

Some kids walk to school.
Some kids ride the bus.

Our small town has one **library**. This is a place to borrow books, movies, and music.

17

Our mayor is the leader of our town. The mayor works at the **town hall**.

Our town has more trees and plants than a big city.

We have a park in our small town. It is a fun place to play with friends!

Words to Know

library

post office

town hall

Index

Websites

Due to the changing nature of Internet links, PowerKids Press has developed an online list of websites related to the subject of this book. This site is updated regularly. Please use this link to access the list: www.powerkidslinks.com/acom/smtwn